Fifteen things
CHARLES AND RAY
teach us

an essay by Keith Yamashita

An essay about the
DESIGNING DUO
that changed how we
look at the world

1:30 P.M.

WEIL

AM

RHEIN,

GERMANY

The grounds of the Vitra Museum
are covered with snow....

Weil am Rhein is a small town, with one road that passes right by the Vitra Design Museum.

The cabdriver drops me at the end of the driveway. I have no idea what he is saying to me. I am hemmed in. A field of snow stretches before me. The road is at my back. Ahead, maybe 150 paces, is the museum.

Small, its arms outstretched and roof angling skyward, this Frank Gehry museum looks lonely out here.

But there, by the entrance, is a huge photo that warms the place. It's of Charles and Ray on a Velocette motorcycle—she at the helm with a determined look to her stance, he as the ebullient passenger warmed by a corduroy jacket and pipe. An unmistakable duo.

Of course, much has been written about them. Charles Ormand Eames. Born in 1907, a self-described "real Midwesterner."

Bernice Alexandra Kaiser—later nicknamed "Ray"—born in 1912 in Sacramento, California. They met at the Cranbrook Academy of Art in 1940. At the time, she was a painting student. He was a professor of architecture. But from that year on, they would never be quite the same. Their partnership would stretch for the next forty years—a career that would take them through furniture, film, toy design, exhibits, architecture and virtually every facet of design.

As you probably know, I am a bit of an Eames nut. Like all of us, I am intrigued by their work. The depth of it. The clarity of it. The whimsy of it. I don't know how many of you will get a chance to make this mecca to this snowy field, so I thought I'd write about what I saw there. Because—as in awe as I thought I'd be— I tell you, I left twice as inspired.

Here are some of the things the Eameses teach us...

No. 1

Keep good company.

FOUR DECADES OF CHRISTMAS CARDS

When you enter the Vitra Museum and wander into the
Eames exhibit, you are instantly confronted by a floor-to-
ceiling wall of vibrant Christmas cards. Pressed between
two pieces of plex are cards from four decades. Hundreds
of cards. Maybe even a thousand cards. All addressed in
some way to the Eameses. Some to Charles. Some to Ray.
Most to both of them. You first notice how colorful the
cards are. Then how they tackle not only the niceties of
holiday greetings—best wishes, Merry Christmas, and
the like—but also the deeper issues of the Cold War era.
Peace. War. Famine. Upon closer examination, you start
to see the signatures on the cards. Oh, there, a Saarinen.
A Rand. A Hoffman. A Nelson. The artists, the designers,
the writers, the architects, the painters, the business
minds who sanctified the profession, brought respect
to the craft through their actions and work.

No. 2

Notice the ordinary.

SNAPSHOTS AND SLIDES

Not too far from the cards is a light table—not unlike any studio's light table, really. But on it, in row after neat row, is a set of 35-mm slides—a collection that is probably rivaled by very few.

And it is strange, because when you peer through the loupe and take a long look at these snapshots, you are struck by something.

These are all pictures of the ordinary.

Railroad tracks. The numbers on the side of a building. A seagull. Some seashells. An **X** on the pavement, calling out a railroad crossing. A manhole cover.

But there is something mysterious captured here, in this collection. How the plain, the commonplace, the mundane make a far more wonderful cast of characters than we give them credit for. You become resolute that you can find that same perfection in your path through the day, maybe even on the way back to the parking lot.

No. 3

Preserve the ephemeral.

RAY'S COLLECTION

Stuff disappears. Charles and Ray didn't let it. That is certainly evident in the fifty-some odd drawers of ephemera that is on display.

You take a look at the long embankment of drawers. Shaker-simple in style—flush, with only a handle on each drawer, no detail otherwise. You pull out one drawer to reveal a set of China dolls—casually composed, almost messy, yet you would not arrange it differently. Another drawer reveals a set of European money—coins, colorful bills, coin wrappers. Another, yarns in rare shades of color. Toys. Leaves. Circus paraphernalia.

You learn here the joys of being a pack rat—but more than that, the importance of preserving ephemeral moments that would otherwise slip away. Forever lost.

No. 4

Design not for the elite, but for the masses.

THE CASE STUDY HOUSES

Along one wall in the downstairs exhibition space is a
set of drawings and floor plans of Charles and Ray's Case
Study House—created for a program sponsored by *Arts &
Architecture* magazine under John Entenza. The purpose
was to design a house for "the postwar way of living."
The design point: an average American worker. Here we
see the Eameses' linear, orderly minds at work. The spaces
within the house are squared off and defined, the floor
plan rectilinear in nature—but at the same time unique,
wonderfully approachable, and livable. In other parts of
the exhibit, too, there is similar evidence of the Eameses'
passion for creating extraordinary experiences for the
masses. Pushing good design into houses, chairs, toys,
tables—all that could be assembled, built, and reproduced
on a grand scale. For cheap. Charles once said, "The
motivation behind most of the things we've done was
we wanted to give them to someone else. And the way
to make that practical is to have the gifts manufactured."

No. 5

Explain it to a child.

TOPS: A FILM

Lots of films are on show here. For instance, *Blacktop,* a film about a schoolground blacktop being washed down by water, and the intriguing patterns of soap and leaves and reflections that result.

Some of the films are observations.

Others teach.

Tops, a film the Eameses completed in 1969, is the one that will mesmerize you. It's a demonstration of the physics of motion. During its seven minutes, fifteen seconds, you learn about the physics of rotational movement—not in a textbook way, but through experience. One young viewer summed up what he got from the film: "Tops are born, they live, and then they die."

Lesson learned.

No. 6

Get lost in the content.

NOTES TO A CALTECH SCIENTIST

The Eameses' desire to understand the subject at hand—
any subject—is admirable. The tougher the subject, the
more ardently they pursued it. You can see that same
determination in the designers in their office, too.

Under glass, there is a trail of correspondence
between a designer in the Eames Office and a scientist
at Caltech. The Eameses were preparing illustrations
for their film *Powers of Ten* (more about this in a minute)
and they needed expert advice on how best to represent
a human cell.

The correspondence is interesting and the sketches
traded amusing, as a young designer reaches out, trying
to master years of cellular biology. The tone is convivial,
humorous, and lighthearted as the designer promises
to make the cell "more blob-ey." And when you see the
film, that cell is utterly believable.

No. 7

Get to the heart of the matter.

IBM PROPOSALS

About halfway through the exhibit you begin to wonder exactly how the Eameses got to do all this great work.

Was it handed to them?

Was it assigned?

Did it come neatly bundled in a creative brief or with some rational strategy?

From the looks of it, no. At least, not what you can see here in this exhibit. Instead you see the Eameses at work conjuring up projects they believed would be in the best interest of their clients. You see the Eameses at their best in their proposals for IBM, certainly their most longstanding patron. In three short pages they outline why management should spend millions to build a museum in Armonk on the IBM campus. The writing is clear and to the point, and describes a place that would have the feeling of a laboratory, where the visitor would be transformed. There is something so honest about the way they explain the idea. Take it or leave it, they seem to say. The idea speaks for itself.

No. 8

Never tolerate "O.K. anything."

A LETTER TO HENRY FORD II

The Eameses drove Fords—maybe a symbol of their
commitment to everyday things. But that is not to
say that they always found them perfect.

 In 1954, they were having a particularly tough
time finding one that suited their needs.

 In a glass case along one wall of the exhibit, you
see two notes. A handwritten draft of a note written
by Charles and Ray about the predicament the couple
found themselves in—and a later one, neatly typed. 23
Frustrated by the process of finding a car without ugly
decor, they were told to write to Henry Ford directly. And
so they did; their doggedness is revealed in their words:

"We find the forced, no-alternative garish decor revolting
and dictatorshiplike."

Their rewrite was more diplomatic, but equally dogged.
The Eameses fought for good design, not just in their own
work, but in the work of others. Maybe there is something
to be learned from that.

No. 9

Remember
your responsibility
as a storyteller.

THE AMERICAN NATIONAL EXHIBITION IN MOSCOW

The year was 1959.

It must have been a doozy of a sight to witness. Seven twenty-by-thirty-foot screens suspended in midair. Twenty-two hundred images of America projected in rapid-fire succession.

George Nelson had selected the Eameses to create this story of America, on behalf of the U.S. government, for the first cultural exchange with the Russian people since the Bolshevik Revolution. This multiple projection system—perhaps the first truly inspired use of "multi-media"—reportedly worked perfectly. The show finished, the crowd was stunned. There was silence. Then deep, lasting applause.

No. 10

Zoom out.

POWERS OF TEN

The Vitra Museum has two floors. On the second floor, you find the gem of the exhibit.

Along three walls are framed all the special effects artwork for *Powers of Ten*—the Eames film about "the relative size of things in the universe and the effect of adding another zero." I realize now that this film was the first thing I must have encountered of the Eameses, and that was in the third grade at Wallace Elementary School in California. I vividly remember this film, even though nearly three decades have passed.

A couple lies on a picnic blanket. The camera zooms out—1 meter away (10^0 meters), then 10 meters (10^1 meters), then 100 meters (10^2 meters), and so on, and so on, until we are one billion light years away.

What amazes me now, looking at the paintings and sets they used in the film, was how good the Eameses were at manipulating, tugging at, and seeing frameworks not as confining constructs, but as a playful means to understanding our world.

No. 11

Switch.

THE EAMESES' PROCLIVITY FOR VARIETY

Never get bored, the work seems to say. Do not fall prey to the narrow label of being a designer. A house. A film. A child's lesson. A chair. All need your talent and skill. Was it that the Eameses were more talented, or merely less focused on the rules of the game?

29

No. 12

Prototype it.

EAMES CHAIRS

"Will it work?"

On the downstairs floor, in the center of the exhibit, is a noisy machine. A large barrel-like beast that rotates, not unlike a huge clothes dryer. Inside is a chair, tumbling away.

It was something the Eameses conjured up to test the durability of their wares. The Eameses, it seems, were big on prototyping.

Nearby, we see a dozen models of the chairs that made Charles and Ray household names.

We see their mock-ups for Herman Miller brochures about their chairs—part information graphics, part sell, part photographic art.

We see the sketches for the aluminum label, designed by the duo, complete with Charles' signature, that went on the bottom of each piece of furniture.

We see their obsession with testing every detail of these chairs. One idea at a time.

No. 13

Pun.

A NOTE FROM CHARLES TO LUCIA, HIS DAUGHTER

While on trips, Charles would write letters to Lucia—little anecdotes about their trip. One particularly stands out.

It's a page-long rebus. On regular lined paper is a series of sketched objects that work together to form a sentence, and then another, and then another. Charles borrows the sound of some words, and slams them against the initials of another.

But what is perhaps most amusing in this game of puns and mindplay is how he signs the letter. He has two letter L's, charred, having just been extinguished: a wisp of smoke spirals skyward.

No. 14

Make design your life. (And life, your design.)

THE DESIGNING DUO

To be admired: longevity, perseverance, joy in the design of commonplace things, finding fuel in the process of discovery, believing that design is a worthy profession that can bring good to people's lives, and being part of any design partnership (let alone relationship) that stretches for this long.

35

No. 15

Leave something behind.

IN THE WORDS OF OTHERS

The very last thing you see is a video documentary by Eames Demetrios, the grandson of Charles and Ray. He has interviewed friends, colleagues, teammates, and other professionals about the work of the couple.

In the words of those who were interviewed, you hear a kind of respect for the duo and what they achieved. And you realize what a legacy they left behind—whether intentionally or not—as it lives through the people they touched and worked with.

But it is a strange realization, and quite unlike the realization you get when you see great art, or hear the voice of a Nobel laureate, or see a man walk in space. There is something empowering about this realization— not humbling. Something that makes you want to get out there and do something. It makes you believe you *can* do something. It makes you believe it is your duty to leave something good behind.

What will your mark be?

Author Keith Yamashita has had a personal and professional passion for all things Eames—from the landmark Eames House to the playful Christmas cards, from the classic Herman Miller furniture to the film *Powers of Ten*. When the Library of Congress and the Vitra Design Museum opened their long-awaited exhibition—*The Work of Charles and Ray Eames: A Legacy of Invention*—Keith made sure he saw it at its very first venue. There he got to see not only a collection of Eames objects, ideas, images, and media—but also the Eameses' way of looking at the world. He created this book for his friends and colleagues to share that experience.

The Eames Office is pleased to publish this book—one person's insights and perspective on Charles and Ray Eames. We felt that by being both specific and universal, this book grasps, in a marvelous way, the Eames spirit. It's a perfect talisman of the first major retrospective of the Eames work in more than two decades.